Introduction

In the early years of the twentieth century, the world was torn apart by a terrible war. It raged for more than four years before the guns finally fell silent. In the words of the time, it was the 'war to end all wars'.

All wars have names. They often give us clues about who was fighting, as well as where and when the war took place. But the names given to this war are different. It was enough to just call it the 'World War' or the 'Great War', both of which hint at its huge scale. Years later, when the world was at war for a second time, it became known as the First World War – the name we use today.

This was the first war where poisonous chemicals were used as weapons of mass destruction, when **tanks** first rumbled across battlefields, when fighter planes, bombers and **airships** took war into the skies, and when submarines and mighty battleships turned the oceans into killing zones. There had never been a war like it.

The First World War began in Europe and eventually spread to more than 100 countries, across every continent except Antarctica. Even before the first shots were fired, there were signs that war was coming. As countries increased their military strength and took sides against each other, the world edged closer to war.

Then, when a royal prince and his wife were murdered in June 1914, a train of events was set in motion. Four weeks later, war was declared. Some said it would be all over by Christmas. How wrong they were. It took four years of bitter and often futile fighting before peace returned in November 1918.

The cost in human life broke all records. Even today we cannot be sure just how many died, although it is likely to be more than 20 million. Whatever the number, it was too many. A generation of young men had been destroyed and the world would never be the same again.

Europe Divided

The countries of Europe were among the world's leading nations. Britain, Germany and France were three of the richest and most powerful. They had large populations and their busy factories were the workshops of the world, making goods that were sold far and wide. Added to this, they had built worldwide empires. It all seemed so good – what could possibly go wrong?

4

The Franco-Prussian War

Like many wars, there was a long, slow build-up to the start of the First World War in 1914. The story begins with a different war from more than 40 years earlier: the Franco-Prussian War, fought between France and Prussia (modern-day Germany). It lasted only a few months and when it ended in 1871, Prussia was the winner. The border regions of Alsace and Lorraine, which had belonged to France, were seized by Prussia. It was a great blow for France not only to lose the war, but also to lose valuable territory. Although the two sides made peace, France was angry that Alsace and Lorraine had been taken, and hoped that one day they would be given back.

NORWAY

SWED

North Sea

DENMARK

UNITED KINGDOM

HOLLAND

GERMAN EMPIRE

BELGIUM

FRANCE

SWITZERLAND

Atlantic Ocean

ITALY

PORTUGAL

SPAIN

Mediterranean Sea

EUROPE 1914

Allies

Countries that joined the Allies

Central Powers

Countries that joined the Central Powers

Neutral countries

MOROCCO

TUNISIA

ALGERIA

The Central Powers

Germany feared that France would try to retake Alsace and Lorraine. With this in mind, Germany decided to make it as hard as possible for France to succeed. Soon after the Franco-Prussian War ended, Germany signed friendship treaties with Italy and Austria-Hungary (which at that time was one empire ruled by Franz Joseph). These three countries formed the Triple Alliance and agreed to support each other if any of them were attacked by other countries. By doing this, Germany sent a 'hands-off' warning to France. From then on, France knew that if it tried to take Alsace and Lorraine back, Italy and Austria-Hungary would takes sides with Germany.

Together, Germany and Austria-Hungary were known as the Central Powers. This was because they were in the centre of Europe, located between Russia in the east and France and Britain in the west.

The Allied Powers

The **alliance** of Germany, Austria-Hungary and Italy made France and Russia nervous. Both countries felt threatened and were concerned that Germany might invade them. In 1894, France and Russia formed an entente (the French word for 'agreement') of their own. They promised to support each other if either was attacked. In 1904, Britain also made an entente with France, pledging support if Germany attacked. Together, Britain, France and Russia were known as the Triple Entente. Later, when the war broke out, they became the Allied Powers.

Now it was the turn of Germany to be concerned. With Russia on her eastern border and France and Britain to the west, Germany felt surrounded.

5

Kaiser Wilhelm II planned to expand Germany's empire, so he built up its army and navy.

This German cartoon shows the Central Powers of Germany and Austria-Hungary as soldiers, facing Russia to the east and France and Britain to the west.

Gearing Up for War

By forming alliances or agreements among themselves, the countries of Europe had taken the first steps towards war. The next step was to build up their military strength. In the years before fighting broke out, both sides increased the sizes of their armies and navies. They also set about building up the first air forces. An arms race had begun.

Conscripts and Volunteers

Germany had the largest peacetime army. It was a conscript army in which men had to serve for two years in the **infantry**, or three years in the cavalry. After they had finished their training, soldiers returned to their everyday lives. They then became part of the German reserve army. France also had a peacetime conscript army, in which men served for three years.

Conscription ensured that if war broke out, Germany and France could call on large numbers of men. However, conscripts didn't always make the best soldiers – they could be poorly trained and not willing to fight.

In contrast to the conscript armies of Germany and France, Britain had a smaller volunteer army. It was regarded as the most professional army in the world, as men had chosen to enlist – they had not been forced to join.

When hostilities began in 1914, Germany had an army of almost two million men, with a further two million in reserve. France had about 750,000 men in its army, and Britain's army, the smallest, numbered about 250,000.

New recruits of the British army during rifle training on the streets of London.

Warships and Submarines

The clearest sign that an arms race was under way could be seen on the world's oceans. It began when Germany announced that it was to build a fleet of new warships. In response, Britain built bigger, faster and more powerful warships of her own. Britain had always had a strong navy and did not want its supremacy at sea to be challenged by Germany. By 1914, Britain had won the naval race with Germany, and her navy was the world's largest and strongest. As well as warships, the two sides also built up their submarine fleet, and on the eve of war Britain had more submarines than any other nation.

7

Warplanes and Airships

Until the First World War, wars had been fought only on the ground and at sea. This war would be different, as it introduced a new, third field of combat – aerial warfare. When war began, both sides sent the first flimsy planes on reconnaissance missions and then into battle, armed with bombs and machine guns. In 1914, Germany's air force was the largest, equipped with a range of warplanes and huge, gas-filled airships called Zeppelins. France and Britain lagged behind at first, with planes that had less firepower than the German planes.

The French Nieuport 11 was one of the first Allied fighter planes and one of the few aircraft that could counter German air superiority.

The Peace Is Shattered

By early 1914, Europe's nations were on the brink of war. They had made agreements to help each other and had men and weapons ready for action. Politicians spoke about war and articles about war appeared in newspapers. It was the calm before the storm and just a matter of time before something, somewhere, broke the fragile peace.

The Black Hand

Finally an event in Bosnia, a small country in south-east Europe, triggered the start of the First World War. Bosnia had been part of the Austro-Hungarian Empire for many years, but by 1914 some Bosnians wanted to break away. They wanted Bosnia to be an independent nation. A few Bosnians formed a secret terrorist group called the Black Hand. Their aim was to strike a blow at Austria-Hungary, by whatever means they could. When it was announced that Archduke Franz Ferdinand, **heir** to the throne of Austria-Hungary, was to visit Bosnia, the Black Hand group decided to **assassinate** him.

AUSTRIA-HUNGARY

ROMANIA

SERBIA
• Belgrade

BOSNIA
Sarajevo

BULGARIA

Black Sea

MONTENEGRO

ALBANIA

GREECE Aegean
Sea

TURKISH
EMPIRE

Bosnia, a small country between the Austro-Hungarian Empire and the Turkish Empire, was where the fragile peace was shattered on 28 June 1914.

Archduke Franz Ferdinand and his wife, just a few minutes before they were assassinated in Sarajevo.

Failed Bomb Attack

On 28 June 1914, Archduke Franz Ferdinand and his wife, Countess Sophie, arrived in Sarajevo, the capital of Bosnia, by train. They left the station in an open-top car, and headed towards the City Hall to meet the mayor. On the way, a member of the Black Hand group threw a bomb at the car. It bounced off the side and exploded against the car behind, injuring two officers from the Archduke's staff. The would-be assassin was caught and the injured men were taken to hospital. Thinking the danger was over, the Archduke insisted that the visit should carry on.

An Assassin's Bullets

After his meeting at the City Hall, the Archduke asked to be driven to the hospital to visit his injured officers. This was not part of the day's plan. On the way to the hospital, the Archduke's driver made a wrong turn into a narrow street. The car slowed to a stop and a young man stepped forwards and fired two shots at the passengers on the back seat.

The man was Gavrilo Princip. He was 19 years old and a member of the Black Hand group. The bullets from his revolver hit their targets and by the time the driver reached the city hospital, Archduke Franz Ferdinand and Countess Sophie were dead.

Gavrilo Princip's actions were the spark that set off the war. He was captured and died in prison less than four years later.

Countdown to War

At the time of the assassination, Kaiser Wilhelm II, the German emperor, was at a yacht race in the German city of Kiel. He was on board his yacht when a telegram was brought to him with news of the Archduke's murder. The race was cancelled and the Kaiser returned to his palace. He knew that now the fragile peace had been broken it was just a question of when the countries of Europe would declare war on each other.

Europe Goes to War

The assassination of Archduke Franz Ferdinand and Countess Sophie sent a shock wave around Europe. It was no less than an act of terrorism against Austria-Hungary, which had lost its future emperor and empress. There was a swift reaction from Austria-Hungary, which blamed Serbia for being behind the killings.

War Is Declared

Serbia was an independent country, located next to Bosnia. For some time, Serbia had been encouraging Bosnia to break away from Austria-Hungary. The Black Hand terrorist group had its headquarters in Belgrade, the capital of Serbia. In addition to this, Gavrilo Princip had been armed by Serbia with the revolver he used for his attack on the Archduke.

On 23 July 1914, the government of Austria-Hungary sent an ultimatum – a demand – to Serbia. It called on Serbia to admit it was behind the murder of Archduke Franz Ferdinand. Also, Serbia would have to give up its independence and become part of the Austro-Hungarian Empire. These demands were unacceptable to Serbia, and the ultimatum was rejected. Five days later, on 28 July 1914, Austria-Hungary declared war on Serbia. The First World War had finally begun.

Nation Against Nation

It only needed one country to declare war for the alliance system to take over. When Austria-Hungary declared war on Serbia, Russia came to Serbia's aid and put its army on standby. Germany reacted by promising to help Austria-Hungary and on 1 August 1914 it declared war on Russia.

Two days later, on 3 August, Germany invaded Belgium and declared war on France. Because Britain had promised to help France, Britain declared war on Germany on 4 August. Over the next few days, more declarations of war were made – Serbia against Germany, Austria-Hungary against Russia, and Britain and France against Austria-Hungary.

The alliance system had drawn most of Europe into war. Now armies were **mobilised** and troops started moving into position. However, there was a general feeling that it would be a quick war and that it would be all over by Christmas 1914, or Easter 1915 at the latest.

11

Cheering German reservists drive
off to their posts following the
declaration of war and the order
to mobilise the army.

How one British
newspaper reported
the outbreak of war.

The German army in
Brussels, following
their capture of the
city on 20 August 1914.

Neutral Countries

At the start of hostilities, some countries tried to remain neutral. These were Italy, Portugal, Greece, Bulgaria, Romania and Turkey. However, as the war developed, they were caught up in the fighting.

From across the Atlantic Ocean, the United States of America watched as the situation in Europe unfolded. It looked like it was going to be a European war fought on European soil. In August 1914, the USA announced that it would remain a neutral country and would not take sides.

The British Army

The First World War was essentially an infantry war – a war fought by soldiers on the ground. Britain's navy and newly formed air force were also active, but it was the foot soldier on the battlefields of Europe, Africa and Asia who saw most of the fighting. He had the traditional nickname 'Tommy Atkins' or 'Tommy' – an ordinary-sounding name for the common British soldier.

(12) Kitchener's Army

Britain's volunteer army was easily outnumbered by the massive conscript army of Germany. In August 1914, Field Marshal Earl Kitchener launched a public appeal for men to enlist. Within days, 100,000 men had volunteered to join Kitchener's Army, as it was soon known. Thousands more followed over the coming months. They had to be aged 18 and over, though many younger volunteers lied about their age in order to join up. As long as they passed a medical examination, they were given the 'king's shilling' – their first day's pay. They were now in the army for the duration of the war.

Posters were put up to encourage men to enlist. They had slogans, such as 'Your country needs you', 'Britain needs more men', and 'Daddy, what did you do in the Great War?'.

Daddy, what did YOU do in the Great War

British Uniform

British Tommies went off to the First World War wearing khaki-coloured uniform ('khaki' is an Urdu word for 'dust'). The jacket was loose-fitting and had four pockets on the outside with button-down flaps. Men also wore khaki trousers, or kilts if they were from a Scottish regiment.

A knapsack on the back was for food rations, a blanket, a coat and personal items. When fully loaded, a soldier's webbing and kit weighed about 32kg.

A 43cm **bayonet** could be fixed to the end of the rifle. It was carried in a scabbard attached to the belt.

In the early part of the war, soldiers wore khaki peaked caps which offered no head protection at all. By the summer of 1916, steel helmets with a khaki finish had been issued.

Infantry soldiers were issued with a Lee Enfield Mark III rifle, which fired ·303-inch calibre bullets. The rifle's magazine held ten bullets. A trained infantry soldier could fire up to 30 aimed bullets per minute.

At the start of the war, heavy stick grenades were used, but from 1915 soldiers were issued with the smaller, oval Mills bomb. After the safety pin was pulled, the grenade was thrown. It exploded seven seconds later.

Over their jackets, soldiers wore webbing. This was a wide waist belt attached to shoulder straps. On each side of the belt were ammunition pouches, which held 150 rifle bullets. On the front were smaller pouches and places to attach a bayonet, a water bottle and an entrenching tool for digging.

Puttees were worn to protect the lower legs. These were long, narrow strips of khaki cloth, wrapped tightly around the leg from the ankle to just below the knee.

13

British Colonial Forces

Soldiers from the countries of the British Empire fought for Britain. Nearly 1,500,000 troops came from India, and 1,000,000 were from Canada, Australia, New Zealand, South Africa and the West Indies.

The Fighting Begins

Germany had made a secret battle plan before the war actually began. It was devised by General Alfred von Schlieffen and was known as the Schlieffen Plan. The idea was that Germany would invade Belgium and then move across into France to defeat it in a lightning attack. After this, German troops would attack Russia. If everything went according to plan, Germany expected to win the war in a matter of weeks.

A German 'Big Bertha' howitzer in action.

The Invasion of Belgium

A German army of 1,500,000 men invaded Belgium early on 4 August 1914. The small Belgian army of 117,000 men stood little chance of halting the German advance. However, they slowed it down by destroying bridges and railway lines. The Germans reached the city of Liège, which was protected by a ring of 12 forts. For five days the Germans pounded the forts with 'Big Bertha' **howitzers**: huge **artillery** pieces that fired high-explosive **shells**. The last of the forts surrendered on 16 August, and four days later the German army entered Brussels, the capital of Belgium.

Men, horses and equipment continued to arrive in France until Field Marshal Sir John French had around 120,000 soldiers at his command.

British Troops Arrive

Britain entered the war on 4 August. Ten days later the first troops of the British Expeditionary Force (BEF) crossed the English Channel and landed in northeast France. The BEF was led by Field Marshal Sir John French. They crossed the border into Belgium and advanced along the main road that linked Paris and Brussels. Advancing towards them was the German army, on its way to Paris.

Mounted troops from the British 16th Lancers retreat from Mons in the first weeks of the war.

The Battle of Mons

British and German forces clashed at Mons in Belgium on 23 August. The battle was fought along a line that stretched for 43 kilometres either side of the town. The Germans greatly outnumbered the British and attacked with heavy artillery and machine-gun fire. The British held them back and inflicted heavy casualties, but were finally forced to retreat into France, with the German army in pursuit. The British retreat took two weeks and the BEF had to stop several times to battle the Germans as they withdrew.

15

The Invasion of France

The French army had battled the Germans along the French border, but they were also forced into a retreat. By the first week in September, the German army had advanced through northeast France pushing the British, French and Belgian forces back, until Paris was within reach. However, the Germans had made such rapid progress that their supplies couldn't keep up. They had advanced non-stop for 33 days, but were now exhausted and low on food and ammunition. Just 40 kilometres from Paris, the German army came to a halt at the River Marne.

The Eastern Front

Russia had an alliance with France, so when Germany invaded France, Russia sent troops into eastern Germany. This was the last thing the Germans wanted, as they now had to fight on both **fronts** at the same time – the **Western Front** (France) and the **Eastern Front** (Russia). Despite this, after the opening months of war on the Eastern Front, Germany was in command.

The Russian infantry were equipped with model 1891 rifles, which had an internal magazine that held five rounds.

The Russian Army

Russia had a conscript army. In peacetime it numbered some 1,300,000 men, but as war approached its strength was increased. By 1914, Russia had the largest army in Europe, with almost six million men. With such a massive army, there was a feeling that Russia could simply force its way across Europe, defeating everything in its path. Most were infantry soldiers, who fought with rifles and hand grenades. There was also an artillery force equipped with howitzers and big guns.

The Cossacks

Russia was famous for its cavalry troops, known as Cossacks. They scouted ahead of the advancing army and fought on horseback with lances, sabres and rifles. In battle, the first line of Cossacks charged at the enemy with their lances. These were long wooden spears tipped with metal points. Lancers were used to break the enemy lines, after which the bulk of the Cossack cavalry rode in to cut down the enemy with their sabres.

Baltic Sea

Tannenburg

GERMANY • Warsaw RUSSIA

AUSTRIA-HUNGARY

ROMANIA

Black Sea

TURKISH EMPIRE

The front line of the Eastern Front in 1914.

The Battle of Tannenberg

Russian troops began their invasion of eastern Germany on 12 August 1914. Germany responded by sending troops from the Western Front. At first, the German army was pushed back, but as the Russians moved further into Germany, they ran into problems. Their supply line was stretched to the limit and the delivery of supplies to the men at the front slowed down. The Germans interecepted Russian radio messages, discovered their plans and were able to make a counter-attack. The Russian army became trapped, and was defeated at the end of August in the Battle of Tannenburg.

In September, Germany inflicted a second crushing defeat on Russia. In the Battle of the Masurian Lakes, more than 45,000 Russians were captured and Russian forces retreated out of Germany.

17

Russian prisoners of war, following their defeat and capture at Tannenberg. More than 18,000 Russian troops were killed, and 92,000 were captured in this key battle.

Russia Invades Austria-Hungary

At the same time as Russia invaded Germany, its troops crossed the Austria-Hungary border into Galicia (now part of modern Poland and Ukraine). At first, they met with success, seizing land and taking thousands of prisoners. This was until Germany sent soldiers to fight alongside the forces of Austria-Hungary. By the summer of 1915, Russia was forced to retreat from Galicia too.

Russian machine-gunners on the Eastern Front.

Having made a rapid advance into France, the German invasion ground to a halt at the River Marne. Paris, the Germans' objective, was only a day's march away, but in front of them were the French and British forces, determined to defend France's capital city. Germany's Schlieffen Plan for a quick war had been a failure and now a very different type of warfare began.

The First Battle of the Marne

The battle along the River Marne started on the afternoon of 5 September 1914 and lasted for seven days. British and French troops launched a full-scale attack on the invading Germans along a wide front. More than 600 taxi cabs drove to the battlefield from Paris, carrying 6,000 French soldiers to the front.

When a large part of the German army moved to the west, a gap opened up in the middle of their line. Allied forces moved into the gap, splitting the German army in two. The Germans realised their mistake and with supplies running out, they began to retreat.

It was an important victory for the Allies. Paris had been saved and the Germans had been pushed back. About 81,700 French and British soldiers had died, but German losses were far greater, with 220,000 men killed in action.

The Channel Ports

Following their defeat in the First Battle of the Marne, the German forces abandoned the Schlieffen Plan and withdrew north towards the River Aisne, a few miles from the border of Belgium. In their hurry to invade France, the Germans had neglected the ports of Dunkirk, Boulogne and Calais, on the north coast of France. Now British troops were arriving at these ports in growing numbers. The Germans saw that if they were not careful, they would be attacked by British troops coming at them from behind.

Race to the Sea

The Germans acted to defend their positions and a 'race to the sea' across the Flanders region of Belgium began. However, the Allies and the Germans kept pace with each other. By November 1914, both sides had reached the sea. Along the way, they'd built long lines of defences, which now ran from the North Sea coast, south through Flanders and across northeast France. The Western Front had been created.

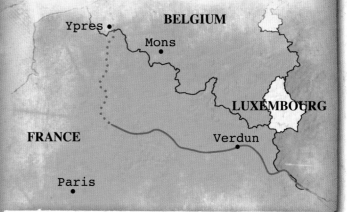

THE WESTERN FRONT 1914

\ **The front line 1914**

∙∙∙ **New fortified trenches built during the 'race to the sea'.**

19

French infantry charge with bayonets fitted at the First Battle of the Marne.

The First Battle of Ypres

In October 1914, the Germans tried to out-move the Allies. They launched an attack, close to the Belgian town of Ypres (say: ee-pruh). In November, after weeks of savage fighting, the First Battle of Ypres ended. The Germans had failed to make a breakthrough, and Ypres remained in Allied hands. Both sides had suffered heavy casualties. This battle marked the end of the opening phase of the war. As Christmas 1914 approached, both sides were dug in along the Western Front.

The French Army

In peacetime, men in France had to join the army for three years of military service. They did this from the age of 20. The system changed when war began in 1914. From then on, men were called up for the length of the war, no matter how long it lasted. It wasn't just men born in France who were **conscripted** into the army – men from France's overseas colonies were also called upon to fight.

New French Uniforms

In 1915, a new uniform was issued in a light blue-grey colour called Horizon Blue and the soft cap was replaced by a steel helmet. Horizon Blue was chosen to match the sky colour of northern Europe. It helped soldiers to blend into the background when seen from a distance, making it harder for the enemy to spot them. The new uniform came with puttees, hard-wearing leather boots and knapsacks to carry equipment in.

Easy Targets

In 1914, during the first year of the war, French soldiers wore colourful uniforms. They dressed in red trousers, dark-blue overcoats and red caps known as kepis (the caps could be covered with a dark-blue cover to make them less obvious). However, the bright colours made them easy targets to spot and as casualties mounted in the opening battles of the war, it was clear that the uniform had to change.

The distinctive red kepi and trousers of the French infantry were gradually replaced by the modern uniform.

A steel combat helmet was issued to French soldiers from June 1915 onwards. It had a crest along the top to help deflect **shrapnel** and a metal badge on the front.

A thin, needle-like bayonet, 52cm long, could be fixed to the end of the rifle. Soldiers gave the bayonet the nickname 'Rosalie'. When not needed, it was carried in a steel scabbard, clipped to the soldier's waist belt. Some troops shortened their bayonets, making them into stabbing knives to use in hand-to-hand fighting.

The Artillery

The French artillery had a powerful weapon in the 75mm field gun. In action, it fired shells at the rate of 15 a minute and had a range of up to 8km. It fired high-explosive and shrapnel shells. The shrapnel shells were packed with hundreds of lead balls, which were flung out in all directions when the shell exploded. The gun proved effective during the First Battle of the Marne in 1914, when it helped to defend Paris. Two years later, at the Battle of Verdun, more than 1,000 French '75s' were in action night and day for eight months, firing 17 million shells at German positions.

The French 75mm field gun needed a team of six horses to pull the gun and an ammunition carrier loaded with 80 shells. A crew of nine men was needed to set up the gun and fire it.

Soldiers of the French infantry were issued with a Lebel Model 1886 rifle, which fired 8mm calibre bullets. The rifle's magazine held eight bullets, and soldiers carried extra ammunition in deep pockets on their coats.

French Colonial Forces

The French army was boosted by about 600,000 soldiers from countries of the French Empire. Most came from the French colonies of Morocco, Algeria and Tunisia, in North Africa, and Senegal, in West Africa. Smaller numbers came from as far away as Vietnam, and the island of Tahiti in the Pacific Ocean. Most had never left their home countries before, and were not used to the cold, damp climate of northern Europe.

Digging In

By Christmas 1914, the war was almost five months old. During this opening phase on the Western Front, the first major battles had been fought and thousands of soldiers had been killed and wounded. Now the armies had come to a stop. A stalemate had been reached and a new type of war began. For the next three and a half years, neither side moved far from their 1914 positions.

Stalemate

A stalemate was reached because both sides had taken up positions in trenches facing each other. **Trenches** and trench warfare defences snaked along the Western Front. There was no way to get around the trenches and they were hard to attack. The trenches stretched about 765 kilometres, from the coast of Belgium, south across France to the border of Switzerland. In mountainous areas, where trenches couldn't be dug, fortified strongholds were built.

The Trench System

The first trenches were little more than lines of pits joined together, but as the network grew the trenches became deeper and were better built, with underground shelters, stores, kitchens and even hospitals. Most trenches were not dug in straight lines, even though this would have been the easiest way to dig them. Instead, they were dug in zigzag lines. This shape offered more protection. If the trench was attacked, men could take cover around the corners and if it was hit by a shell, shrapnel would not be sprayed along the whole length of the trench.

Types of Trench

There were different types of trench. Nearest to the enemy were the front-line firing trenches. Behind these were support trenches where troops rested and waited to move up to the front line. Linking the firing and support trenches were communication trenches for troops to walk to and from the front line.

A wooden handle would be fitted to this British entrenching tool so that it could be swung like a pickaxe when digging.

French soldiers resting in an underground sleeping area within their network of trenches.

No-man's-land

In front of the firing trenches was **no-man's-land**. This narrow strip of ground was all that separated the two sides. It varied in width, but in some places the troops were so close that they could call out to each other from their trenches. Belts of **barbed wire** covered no-man's-land making it difficult and dangerous to cross. Wiring parties entered no-man's-land under the cover of darkness to check, repair and lay barbed wire defences.

If an infantry attack was planned, soldiers went ahead with wire cutters like these to cut paths through the wire.

Christmas Day, 1914

On Christmas Day, 1914, the frozen ground on the Western Front sparkled with frost. Christmas trees appeared along the German trenches and for a few short hours the fighting unexpectedly stopped. Carols were sung, and men from both sides met in no-man's-land to exchange gifts of chocolate and tobacco. They played football and gathered up the bodies of their fallen comrades for burial. At the end of the day the men returned to their positions. The unofficial truce was over and the fighting resumed.

Trench Warfare

The system of trenches along the Western Front brought the two sides dangerously close to each other. Separated only by no-man's-land, the troops were well within firing range of each other's trenches. Soldiers were shot at by snipers, raked by machine gun fire, poisoned by gas and blown up by grenades, **mortars**, shells and other explosives.

Machine Guns

In trench warfare, a decisive weapon on both sides was the machine gun. British troops had the Vickers machine gun, and German troops had the MG08 machine gun. Both were fired in short bursts of about 400 rounds per minute. They had a range of about 1,800 metres, which meant they could reach the enemy trenches on the other side of no-man's-land.

Trench Attacks

When an infantry attack was made on an enemy trench, it usually began with a heavy mortar **bombardment**, which could last for several hours. The mortars then fired smoke bombs to cover no-man's-land in thick, black smoke before the order to advance was given. Soldiers then climbed out of the trenches and went '**over the top**'. As they neared the enemy trench they lobbed hand grenades, which exploded into showers of deadly shrapnel. If they made it into an enemy trench, they fought with pistols, bayonets, knives and clubs.

Trench Hazards

In wet weather, trenches filled with water and the ground turned to mud. Soldiers couldn't keep their feet dry and fell victim to 'trench foot', a condition where their feet became numb, swollen and covered with blisters and sores. In the worst cases, their feet actually started to rot. Rats were a constant menace, and there was always the danger of them spreading disease. Another problem was lice, which attached themselves to the men's bodies and spread quickly between them.

25

Trench Mortars

While machine gun bullets were whizzing over the tops of the trenches, high explosive and shrapnel mortar shells were falling onto them from above. These were fired by trench mortars – rapid-fire weapons that could launch as many as 25 shells per minute. The Germans called them 'bomb-throwers'. Towards the end of the war, the British army had 3,000 mortars on the Western Front, which kept up a constant **barrage**.

War Underground

Because it was so dangerous to cross no-man's-land to attack, both sides began to tunnel underneath it. Deep below the surface, teams of sappers (miners) dug towards each other's trenches. It was dangerous work, as there was the constant risk of the tunnel collapsing, flooding, or being discovered by the other side. When the tunnel was under the enemy trench, it was packed with tons of high explosives. These made the biggest explosions of the war, leaving giant craters in the ground and destroying large sections of trenches.

The Great Guns

Far behind the trenches on the Western Front were the long-range artillery pieces. These were the big guns of war, firing shells onto enemy positions across no-man's-land. At times of heavy fighting there was a constant booming sound as field guns and howitzers released their shells. An artillery barrage could last for days and often came before an attack by the infantry.

Howitzers

A very different type of big gun called a howitzer was developed to attack the trenches. It had a short barrel and fired shells at a steep angle. The shells fell straight down onto the enemy trenches across no-man's-land. As the war went on, howitzers became bigger and more powerful, until tractors and even trains were needed to move some of them into position.

Field Guns

At the start of the war, field guns were the main pieces of heavy artillery. These were traditional artillery weapons with long barrels, best suited to battles fought across large areas of open ground. However, field guns had little effect against the trenches of the Western Front. This was because they were designed to fire shells at a low angle over the ground. Their shells simply skimmed over the top of the trenches and landed far behind enemy lines.

A German 'Big Bertha' howitzer as used in the bombardment of the Belgian forts at Liège.

Artillery Tactics

A barrage usually began with a brief but heavy bombardment of the enemy lines. The big guns would fire high explosive and shrapnel shells. Within minutes, thousands of shells would explode along the enemy front line.

Following this, the artillery changed tactics and began firing a 'creeping barrage'. They aimed their shells to explode in a long line in front of their own infantry troops as they advanced across no-man's-land. Each volley of shells crept forward by about 50 metres at a time, with the troops advancing behind it. Eventually, the creeping barrage reached the enemy trenches. Here, the bombardment stopped and the troops engaged the enemy in close-range fighting.

A creeping barrage was risky for the infantry. Soldiers crossing no-man's-land could be killed by 'friendly fire' if they advanced too fast and walked into the path of shells fired by their own side. There was also a risk that the gunners might misjudge the distance and bombard their own men.

Big Bertha Howitzer

The 'Big Bertha' was a type of German super-heavy howitzer – one of the biggest of the war. It fired high-explosive shells, each weighing about 900kg. Big Berthas proved themselves in the first days of the war as they smashed down the Belgian forts at Liège. The forts' thick walls could withstand an attack from the front by field guns, but they could not survive being bombarded from above. Giant shells from the Big Berthas landed on top of the forts and they were blown to pieces.

The German Army

Germany believed in the idea of 'a nation at arms'. This meant that if war broke out, a large part of the population would already be trained and ready to fight. For many years before the war, every able-bodied German man between the ages of 17 and 45 did military service. When the war began, Germany had the largest of all the armies, with almost two million men. There were as many again in reserve, waiting to be called up.

The *pickelhaube* gave little protection from bullets and shrapnel, so in 1916, soldiers were issued with a harder helmet made from steel.

Infantry Uniforms

German infantry soldiers wore grey jackets and trousers that were tucked into leather boots that came to just below the knee. Equipment belts around their waists carried ammunition pouches, bayonets, spades and axes, and on their backs were knapsacks. At the start of the war, German soldiers were issued with a highly distinctive helmet known as a *pickelhaube* (spiked helmet). It was made from hard leather and had a spike on top to deflect blows from cavalry swords.

Stormtroopers

Stormtroopers were the elite fighting men of the German army. They were the army's best soldiers, and were hand-picked from other infantry units. They were trained as assault troops, and it was their job to 'storm' through enemy lines without stopping. Stormtroopers were well equipped, moved fast, and thought of themselves as the 'princes of the trenches'.

German stormtroopers armed with a flamethrower.

For hand-to-hand fighting a bayonet 65cm long could be fixed to the end of the Mauser rifle. This made it the the same length as the French Lebel rifle

German infantrymen threw stick grenades with an explosive charge in a metal case at the end of a wooden throwing handle. British troops nicknamed them 'potato mashers' because of their shape. Although a stick grenade was heavy, a good thrower could throw one about 35 metres. It exploded about five seconds after it was thrown. If it landed on high ground, its shape stopped it from rolling back towards the thrower.

The Mauser was the standard rifle of the German infantry. The magazine held five bullets. It was an accurate rifle with a range of about 790 metres. Regular infantry were issued with the long-barrelled Mauser, but Stormtroopers were given a short-barreled version, which was lighter and easier to handle in a fast-moving attack.

The Austro-Hungarian Army

The army of Austria-Hungary, like that of Germany, was a conscript force. When the war began it numbered almost two million men, conscripted from eleven different countries within the Austro-Hungarian empire. Infantry soldiers wore a grey-coloured uniform, similar to the uniform worn by German soldiers, usually with a peaked cap. Cavalry units, known as Uhlans, wore light blue jackets and red breeches, often with tall caps.

Trench warfare meant that Austro-Hungarian Uhlans had to adapt to fighting on foot.

The Gallipoli Campaign

Turkey entered the war in late October 1914, on the side of the Central Powers (Germany and Austria-Hungary). Within weeks, the Turkish army went northwards to attack Russian troops in the Caucasus, a mountainous region between the Black Sea and the Caspian Sea. Russia asked for help, and Allied troops were sent to fight in Turkey.

The Dardanelles

Turkey posed a threat to the British navy's oil supplies in the Middle East. Britain and France came up with a plan to seize the Dardanelles – a narrow sea passage that separated Europe from Asia. It belonged to Turkey. If the Allied plan worked, and they took control of this important sea lane, they could then strike at Constantinople (present-day Istanbul), the capital of the Turkish Empire. If Constantinople fell, Turkey would be knocked out of the war.

Aegean Sea

British landing

GALLIPOLI

The Dardanelles

Anzac landing

British landing

TURKISH EMPIRE

The Allies Attack

The Allied attack began in February 1915, when British and French warships bombarded Turkish forts along the coast of the Dardanelles. In mid-March, the fleet sailed along the strait, but the attack failed when several ships were destroyed by Turkish mines. It was clear that Turkey was not going to be defeated by naval power alone – land forces would also be needed.

Australian troops at Gallipoli advance uphill with their bayonets fixed.

Trapped on the Beaches

The Gallipoli campaign went wrong from the start. Supply ships were delayed and when the Anzac troop ships arrived, instead of landing on a gently sloping beach as planned, the current forced them on to an area of cliffs. The Anzacs went ashore and were pinned down by heavy fire from Turkish troops firing from the cliffs above. British troops came ashore at five beaches and were also trapped by Turkish fire. Instead of a rapid advance across the Gallipoli peninsula, Allied troops became stuck on its beaches and coastal cliffs.

The Allied troops at Gallipoli were forced to dig themselves into trenches, just like troops on the Western Front.

Anzacs Sent To Gallipoli

In April 1915, 75,000 Allied infantry troops were sent to the Gallipoli peninsula, Turkey. It was a long finger of land with the Dardanelles on one side and the Aegean Sea on the other. Most of the Allied troops came from Britain, India and France, but there were also a large number of soldiers from Australia and New Zealand, who were known as 'Anzacs'. Gallipoli was the first major military action fought by Australia and New Zealand during the war.

Secret Evacuation

In August 1915, 20,000 fresh Allied troops were sent to Gallipoli to break the deadlock, but the Turkish forces pushed them back. As winter approached and Allied troops began to die of cold and disease, orders were given to evacuate Gallipoli. The evacuation was done in great secrecy at night. In the daytime, troops moved up and down the trenches, firing rifles from all along the front to trick the Turks into thinking the trenches were still fully manned. By January 1916 the last troops had been rescued from the beaches. Not a single man was killed during the evacuation, but in the nine months of fighting the failed Gallipoli campaign had cost the lives of 53,000 Allied and as many as 80,000 Turkish troops. Of the Anzacs at Gallipoli, 8,700 Australians and 2,721 New Zealanders died.

The War at Sea

Britain and Germany had the largest and strongest navies in the world. Britain had the most ships, but the German ships were newer, better armed and had thicker armour. For the first eighteen months of the war, the two sides kept their distance. While the British navy **blockaded** Germany, stopping merchant ships from getting through, the German navy concentrated on submarine warfare. When the sides finally clashed in 1916, it was the biggest sea battle of the war.

Submarine Warfare

The greatest threat to Allied ships came from Germany's fleet of *Unterseebooten* (undersea boats). The British called these German submarines 'U-boats'. U-boats patrolled the North Atlantic, the waters around Britain, and the Mediterranean Sea on the lookout for merchant ships. They were armed with a deck gun and torpedoes. The worst period for U-boat attacks was the spring of 1917, when they sank about 800 merchant ships a month.

U-boats could stay at sea for about four weeks. Most of the time they cruised along on the surface, as this meant they used less fuel and the crew had fresh air to breathe.

The Sinking of the Lusitania

On 7 May, 1915, the passenger liner *Lusitania* was nearing the end of her voyage from New York, USA, to Liverpool, England. On board were 1,962 passengers and crew. As the ship passed the coast of southern Ireland, it was hit by a **torpedo** from a German submarine. She sank in just 18 minutes, and 1,200 people drowned. Germany claimed the *Lusitania* was armed and carried troops and ammunition, which made it a fair target. However, *Lusitania* was in fact a defenceless passenger ship and the sinking caused widespread outrage against Germany.

Battle of Jutland

At the end of May 1916, the German navy sailed into the North Sea. The plan was to attack merchant ships in order to lure part of the British fleet into a trap. The Germans hoped to destroy British warships, before escaping back to their bases in Germany. However, the British knew about the German plan and were prepared for battle. The fleets met off the coast of Denmark – a total of about 250 battleships, battlecruisers, cruisers, destroyers and other ships. Both sides lost ships and thousands of men, but there was no clear winner. The German fleet retreated to its home ports, while the British fleet returned to patrolling the North Sea and escorting merchant ships.

Camouflage patterns created an optical illusion that made it difficult for U-boats to work out a merchant ship's course and to aim torpedoes at it.

HMS *Lion* (left) under fire while HMS *Queen Mary* (right) is blown up by German shells at the Battle of Jutland.

Convoys and Camouflage

Britain responded to the U-boat attacks by putting its merchant ships into groups known as convoys. As many as 50 ships sailed together, escorted by destroyers. If a U-boat was seen, the destroyers attacked it. Another tactic was camouflage. Merchant ships were painted with patterns such as black and white stripes and diamonds. Convoys and camouflage worked, and in 1918 the U-boats only sank 134 Allied merchant ships.

War in Africa

Britain, France, Belgium and Germany had colonies in Africa. They might have been far away from the fighting in Europe, but they were drawn into the war too. Germany had four colonies in Africa, with military bases, radio stations and supplies that could be used against the Allies. The Allied Powers wanted to seize Germany's colonies, to take them out of the war.

Conflict in West Africa

Within days of the war starting in Europe, the conflict spread to the German colony of Togoland, a tiny colony surrounded by British and French territories. At the end of August 1914, Allied forces invaded. There was no resistance. The Germans destroyed their new radio station to prevent it being seized by the Allies, then they surrendered.

AFRICA 1914

French colonies

German colonies

British colonies

TOGOLAND

CAMEROON

BRITISH EAST AFRICA

Dar-es-Salaam

GERMAN EAST AFRICA

GERMAN SOUTH WEST AFRICA   Windhoek

SOUTH AFRICA

Germans captured by the British troops in Togoland being marched off as prisoners of war.

More German Colonies Fall

Next to come under Allied attack was the German colony of Cameroon, a large territory the size of Germany and France combined. British, French and Belgian forces invaded in August 1914 and met with strong resistance from a large garrison of German and African troops. The British navy then captured ports on the Atlantic coast. When the capital and radio station were taken, the Germans retreated to the mountainous inland region. After a lengthy campaign, Cameroon surrendered to the Allies in February 1916.

The third German colony was German South West Africa (present-day Namibia). When the war began, the Germans abandoned their bases along the Atlantic coast and moved inland to the capital, Windhoek. From there, they sent raiding parties into South Africa. This action brought South Africa into the war. The German raiders were pushed back, and in July 1915, the colony of German South West Africa surrendered.

The Struggle for East Africa

The fighting in German East Africa (present-day Tanzania) was the fiercest and longest of the war in Africa. The colony was the size of France and it was Germany's most important territory in Africa. Britain was determined to capture it, as it posed a serious threat to British East Africa (present-day Kenya). Hostilities began on 8 August 1914, when a British battleship bombarded Dar-es-Salaam, the capital of German East Africa. A landing party went ashore and destroyed a German radio station. But if the Allies thought that German East Africa would be quick to surrender, they were wrong.

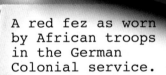

A red fez as worn by African troops in the German Colonial service.

Guerilla Warfare

The Germans, supported by colonial African troops, defeated invading British and Indian forces, whose weapons and ammunition they captured. The Germans began to use guerilla tactics, carrying out highly effective raids, ambushes and acts of sabotage, before disappearing back into the forests, hills and river valleys of the region. It turned into a long campaign that outlasted the war in Europe, until the Germans finally surrendered on 23 November 1918.

In four years of conflict, the East African campaign claimed the lives of about 12,000 soldiers and 365,000 civilians and **non-combatants** who were caught up in the fighting.

British colonial forces in East Africa included the King's African Rifles (above), who wore a fez as part of their uniform.

British colonial troops from India, taken prisoner by the Germans following their victory in the Battle of Tanga, German East Africa, November 1914.

This German poster shows General von Lettow-Vorbeck, who remained undefeated in the campaign against the British in East Africa.

Chemical Warfare

Late in the afternoon of 22 April 1915, the wind blew a cloud of greenish-yellow gas across a section of the Western Front. It came from the German front line, near the Belgian town of Ypres, and moved steadily towards the Allied trenches on the other side of no-man's-land. It was a deadly new weapon – poison gas.

The First Gas Attack

The first gas attack on the Western Front was made on the first day of the Second Battle of Ypres. The Germans took about 5,700 metal cylinders filled with **chlorine** gas to their front line trenches and spaced them out over a distance of 6.5 kilometres. When the weather conditions were just right, the gas was released. Because the chlorine gas was heavier than air, it didn't float away. Instead, it sank to the ground and was carried by the wind towards the French, Canadian and Algerian troops in their trenches.

As the cloud of chlorine gas rolled over the Allied lines and dropped down into their trenches, the unsuspecting men breathed it in. It burned their lungs, making them gasp for air. Their eyes watered and they were blinded. In the confusion, many men climbed out of the gas-filled trenches and began to run, only to be shot down by German gunfire.

The attack lasted for about ten minutes, before the wind dispersed the deadly cloud. In that short time, about 6,000 men died and a wide gap was opened up in the Allied front-line. The Germans had a brief chance to quickly advance and break through the Allied positions, but they were worried that there might still be gas in the area. They advanced too slowly and the Allies had time to regroup and defend their lines.

Protection from Gas

The men who were exposed to that first cloud of poisonous chlorine gas had no protection against it. In desperation, some held water- or urine-soaked cloths to their mouth and nose. They hoped these wet cloths would remove the poisonous chlorine, because it dissolves in water.

Soon after the gas atack at Ypres, cotton pads dipped in bicarbonate of soda were rushed to British troops on the front line for them to breathe through. Later, they were issued with gas masks that covered the whole of the face. At the first sign of a gas attack, whistles or rattles were sounded and the men pulled their masks on.

German soldiers wearing gas masks advance through clouds of gas during an attack.

British gas mask caption image.

Mustard Gas

In 1917, the Germans began using a new chemical weapon – mustard gas. Unlike chlorine gas which depended on the wind to blow it across the battlefield, mustard gas could be put into shells and fired from guns. It was a liquid gas that turned to vapour on impact, causing skin blisters and blindness on soldiers who came into contact with it. Since mustard gas stayed active in the ground for weeks, it created dangerous no-go areas where soldiers risked being contaminated. Both sides used artillery to fire shells filled with deadly poison gas.

A British gas mask. As air was breathed in, it passed through a layer of charcoal that filtered out the gas.

French soldiers loading a gas shell into a howitzer.

The Battle of Loos

On 25 September 1915, during the Battle of Loos, the British used chlorine gas for the first time. It was released from more than 5,200 cylinders and killed 600 Germans in their trenches. Unfortunately for the British, the gas wasn't completely blown over to the German lines. This meant that the British soldiers had to advance through the gas cloud that still blanketed no-man's-land. Many fell victim to the gas meant for the enemy.

British soldiers blinded by gas are led to a casualty station for treatment.

British troops moving into a cloud of chlorine gas at Loos.

Italy Enters the War

When the war began, it was expected that Italy would take sides with Germany and Austria-Hungary, as the three countries had formed the Triple Alliance (see page 5). However, Italy decided to stay out of the fighting and remain a neutral country. But, ten months into the war, Italy finally joined the conflict on the side of the Allies.

Italian Alpine troops climbing a rock face. The mountainous Alps made the movements of troops and equipment slow and dangerous.

War in the Mountains

On 23 May 1915, Italy declared war on her former ally, Austria-Hungary. Italy's reason for declaring war was to gain territory. Italy planned to seize areas in the south of the Austro-Hungarian Empire, where Italian was the main language spoken. It was a mountainous region at the foot of the Alps – the highest mountains in Europe. Austria-Hungary was determined to defend its territory and because it controlled the mountains, it meant that the Italians had to fight their way uphill. Snow and deadly avalanches added to their difficulties.

The Italian Front

The Italians thought they would quickly defeat Austria-Hungary. At first it looked as if they would, because in June 1915 they made a rapid advance into Austria-Hungary along a front line that stretched for 650km. However, after this initial success, all hope of a rapid victory disappeared, as Austria-Hungary fought off the Italians.

AUSTRIA-HUNGARY

SWITZERLAND

Alps

Caporetto
Isonzo

ITALY

ITALY 1915

Twelve Battles of the Isonzo

Much of the action on the Italian Front was in the east, along the valley of the River Isonzo. There was almost continuous fighting there for two years, from 1915 to 1917. Twelve battles were fought, known today as the Battles of the Isonzo. The most successful battle for Italy was the Sixth Battle of the Isonzo, fought in August 1916, in which Italian troops captured the town of Gorizia.

Thinking they were well on the way to defeating Austria-Hungary, the Italian government declared war on Germany, on 28 August 1916. This was a mistake. The Italians expected the British and French to send troops to help them fight Germany, but the Allies had none to spare. Italy then had to fight the combined forces of Austria-Hungary and Germany on her own.

Italian troops take cover in a trench dug into a limestone plateau in the Alps.

Battle of Caporetto

The Twelfth Battle of the Isonzo, also known as the Battle of Caporetto, was fought high up in the mountains in October and November 1917. It began with an intense German artillery bombardment. Shells filled with poison gas were fired at the Italian lines. There were many casualties, as the Italians wore old-fashioned gas masks that hardly worked.

On the second day of the battle, the mountains were shrouded in cloud and there was snow on the ground. In the bad weather the Germans and Austro-Hungarians mounted a surprise attack and pushed through the centre of the Italian line. The Italians retreated down the mountains, destroying bridges as they went. They were chased all the way. After 11 days, the Austro-Hungarians and Germans had advanced 130 kilometres into Italy, capturing prisoners and seizing large quantities of guns and ammunition as they went.

The battle was a crushing defeat for Italy and a blow for the Allies. As a result, Britain and France sent troops to strengthen the Italian front line and the German and Austro-Hungarian advance was eventually halted.

Some of the 275,000 Italian troops that were taken prisoner following their defeat at Caporetto.

War in the Air

On the night of 25 August 1914, a German airship floated quietly over the Belgian city of Antwerp. It dropped nine bombs, killing civilians and damaging buildings. This was the first bombing raid of the war and showed the growing importance of air forces. As the war progressed, both sides built up fleets of airships and aeroplanes for spotting the enemy and for aerial warfare.

Zeppelins were also used by the German navy to search for Allied ships.

Airships

Airships were filled with hydrogen gas and because this was lighter than air they floated. Beneath their fabric outer layer was a rigid metal frame that held several large inflatable bags – like balloons – that were filled with hydrogen gas. On the outside were cabins for the crew and passengers, as well as the propeller engines that moved the airship along.

The airships of Germany were the biggest and most advanced. In Germany, they were known as Zeppelins, after their designer Ferdinand von Zeppelin. During the war, Zeppelins were used as long-range bombers, bringing terror to towns and cities far from the front-line fighting. The first Zeppelin raid on Britain came in January 1915, when two Zeppelins bombed towns on the east coast of England. That May, the first bombs were dropped on London from a Zeppelin, and by 1918 more than 5,000 bombs had fallen on towns across Britain.

Aeroplanes

Aeroplanes were a new weapon of war. They were small, propeller-driven flying machines with open cockpits. At the start of the war, they were mainly used for reconnaissance flights. Pilots flew over enemy territory, while an observer made notes and photographed the positions of enemy troops and weapons. As the war in the air went on, aeroplanes were developed for bombing, air-to-air combat and for ground attacks.

Both sides developed fighter planes for aerial combat, such as the British Sopwith Pup (top) and the German Albatros DIII (bottom).

Fighter Planes

By 1915, the first specialised fighter planes had been developed, fitted with machine guns that could be fired by the pilot. French designers found a way for the machine gun's bullets to be fired through the spinning propeller without damaging it. When a French plane was shot down behind enemy lines, the Germans discovered the secret and began to use it on their fighter planes. For a time, German fighters were the best there were, but by 1917 French and British fighters had been developed that could match them.

41

Bomber Planes

The first bombers were actually scout planes, where the bombs were artillery shells thrown from the cockpit by hand. By 1915, the first purpose-built bombers had taken to the skies. Allied bombers dropped bombs onto German industrial sites and railway stations. In 1917, Germany's bombers began flying on long-range bombing raids against London.

German ground crew load a 100kg bomb underneath a Gotha bomber. These flew long-range bombing missions, usually at night.

The German 'Flying Circus'

In the first years of the war, fighter pilots flew alone, scouring the skies for enemy planes to attack. Tactics changed in the autumn of 1916, when German fighters began flying together in groups. The most famous of the German hunter squadrons was led by Manfred von Richthofen. It became known as 'The Flying Circus' because of the bright colours of its aircraft. Richthofen had his plane painted red, which earned him the nickname 'The Red Baron'. He was the leading fighter pilot of the war, having shot down a total of 80 Allied planes.

1916: a Year of Battles

As 1916 began, the war along the Western Front had reached deadlock. Since the end of 1914, both sides had been dug into their trenches, which made it very difficult for either side to win an outright victory over the other. It had become a siege war and both sides planned to break through and to end the **stalemate**.

The Battle of Verdun

Germany made the first move to gain ground on the Western Front. On 21 February 1916, the Germans began a massive bombardment of the fortified French city of Verdun. For twelve hours, more than two million shells rained down on the French positions. Then the German infantry advanced, moving in behind a creeping barrage of artillery fire (see page 27). Thousands of French soldiers were taken prisoner and thousands more retreated. The German advance continued until the forts had been taken. For a moment, it looked as if victory at Verdun was within their grasp.

The French Lifeline

However, the Germans had not counted on the determination of the French, who fought back ferociously. More French troops and artillery pieces were sent to Verdun along the only remaining road. For the first time in warfare, convoys of motorized trucks were used instead of horses to move men and supplies to the front. The road was Verdun's lifeline and was known as the 'Sacred Way'.

Counter-Attacks

By the middle of April, French gunners had knocked out the German heavy guns. Gradually, French forces retook the ground that had been lost. They made a series of counter-attacks and in mid-December the German army retreated from Verdun. The battle had raged for ten months – it was the longest battle of the war. The death toll was enormous, with 700,000 men killed in action.

German troops in their trenches await the order to attack at Verdun.

French gunners moving a heavy howitzer in the woods at Verdun, September 1916.

A British soldier rescues a wounded comrade on the first day of the Battle of the Somme.

The Battle of the Somme

On the 24 June, British artillery began a week-long intensive bombardment of the German lines. One and a half million shells were fired to destroy the German barbed wire, guns and trenches before the infantry advanced. Then, on the morning of 1 July, huge mines planted deep beneath some of the German trenches were detonated, blowing everything above them to pieces. The order to advance was given and thousands of British and French soldiers rose up out of the front-line trenches. They began to walk across no-man's-land, which was still shrouded in smoke from the shelling.

As they struggled through the barbed wire and shell holes, it became clear that the bombardment had failed. German troops emerged from their deep dugouts and met the Allied troops with a hail of machine gun fire. Within an hour, thousands lay dead or dying on the battlefield. By the end of the first day of the Battle of the Somme, there were 60,000 British casualties, including 20,000 dead. It was the worst day's losses in the history of the British army.

The Big Push

In the summer of 1916, while the Battle of Verdun was still being fought, the British Expeditionary Force and the French army launched a huge attack against the Germans in northern France. This was the Battle of the Somme, fought on either side of the River Somme. For the British, this was to be an all-out attack. They called it the 'Big Push'.

German machine gunners fired a deadly hail of bullets at the advancing Allied soldiers.

Heavy Losses

The battle continued on and off until November 1916. New troops poured in from Britain and France, but also from Australia, New Zealand, Canada, Newfoundland and South Africa. However, the 'Big Push' never came and after almost five months of fighting, the Allies had only advanced 10km. Both sides had suffered heavy losses. More than 300,000 men had been killed in action and 780,000 had been wounded.

The First Tanks

Tanks were first used on the Western Front, during the Battle of the Somme. They were a top-secret British weapon. On 15 September 1916, 36 tanks drove slowly across no-man's-land towards the German lines. Machine gun bullets simply bounced off them. The tanks flattened the barriers of barbed wire and filled the German trenches with gunfire from end to end. This powerful new weapon raised hopes for a breakthrough on the Western Front and changed the face of warfare forever.

A New Weapon

The British needed a weapon to break the deadlock on the Western Front. The plan was to build an armoured vehicle that could cross the enemy's barbed wire and trenches. It would act as a shield for infantry advancing across no-man's-land. The vehicle was to be known as a '**land ship**', but the workers who made it called it a 'tank' because it reminded them of a metal water tank. The nickname stuck and Mark I tanks reached France in the first months of 1916.

The Mark I tank needed a crew of eight. Each man was equipped with two gas masks, a leather helmet to protect against bumps, goggles, a revolver, a haversack and medical kit. In addition to this equipment, the tank was loaded with tins of food, loaves of bread, a spare machine gun, 33,000 rounds of machine gun ammunition, 300 cannon shells, drums of oil and grease, signalling flags and a telephone device. There was even a basket of carrier-pigeons, ready to fly back to base with messages tied to their legs.

As the war progressed, the role of tanks changed. Instead of supporting the infantry, they led it into battle. Tank design improved, and they were fitted with bigger guns, thicker armour and were operated by larger crews.

A British Mark IV tank in action at the Battle of Cambrai, France, 1917.

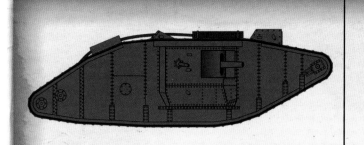

The British Mark I Tank

Powered by a tractor engine, the Mark I tank crawled along on caterpillar tracks at a steady speed of six kilometres per hour – roughly the same as the walking speed of a person. It weighed about 28 tonnes and was covered in heavy steel armour plates to protect the crew inside from bullets. The Mark I was armed with cannons and machine guns.

The German A7V Tank

The German army was slow to develop its own tank. At first, the Germans simply used captured British tanks. In 1918, Germany finally built a tank of its own, but only 20 were ever built. The German A7V tank was a heavy, box-like vehicle with a crew of 18. Each tank was given a name, such as Siegfried, Lotti or Mephisto. The German tank proved to be unreliable and was quick to break down.

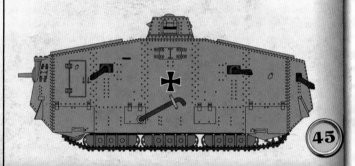

The First Tank Battle

The first tank against tank battle in history took place near Villers-Bretonneux on the Western Front on 24 April 1918. Three German A7V tanks were advancing when they met three British Mark IV tanks. The German tanks used armour-piercing bullets, which smashed through the hulls of two of the British tanks. The damaged tanks retreated. The remaining British tank fired on one of the German tanks and disabled it. The Mark IV then opened fire on the other two German tanks and they retreated. As the British tank moved back to safer ground, it was hit by a mortar shell which damaged its tracks. The crew abandoned it, and escaped into a British trench.

The German A7V tank 'Mephisto', captured by Australian troops during the battle near Villers-Bretonneux.

America Joins the War

At the start of the war, the United States of America remained neutral, but, as the months passed, it could not avoid getting caught up in the conflict. A major incident was the sinking of the *Lusitania* liner in 1915 by a German submarine (see page 32). Many American passengers drowned, which led to anti-German protests in America. Because Germany wanted to keep America out of the war, it promised to stop attacking merchant ships without warning. Germany kept its promise until 1917.

German sailors keep a lookout from the conning tower of a U-boat.

A German Plot Uncovered

In January 1917, a top-secret German message was decoded by British codebreakers. British officials handed it over to the United States government. It revealed that the Germans wanted Mexico to enter the war on the side of Germany by declaring war against the United States. In return for Mexico's support, Germany promised to hand back Texas, Arizona and New Mexico (American states that had once been part of Mexico). The Mexican president refused to do as the Germans asked and Mexico remained a neutral country. The telegram also revealed that Germany planned to secretly resume its submarine attacks on merchant ships. In America, the reaction was one of outrage.

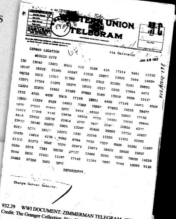

932.29   WWI DOCUMENT: ZIMMERMAN TELEGRAM, 1917.
Credit: The Granger Collection, New York

The coded telegram sent to the German ambassador in Mexico was a major factor in America joining the war.

Submarine Warfare Resumes

In January 1917, Germany announced that it was going to start attacking merchant ships again. German submarines were given orders to sink as many merchant ships as they could. The plan was to stop supply ships carrying food from reaching Britain. The Germans had worked out that without regular shipments of food from overseas, the British people would face starvation within months. They hoped this would force Britain to surrender. Many of the supply ships were American and eight were quickly sunk by German submarines.

New recruits during bayonet drill in an American training camp.

America Declares War on Germany

America could no longer stay out of the war. On 6 April 1917, the United States declared war on Germany. Later, war was also declared on Austria-Hungary, Turkey and Bulgaria. The American army prepared to leave for Europe. In June 1917, the first American troops arrived in France. By the summer of 1918, America was sending 10,000 soldiers to France every day. The American navy's battleships and submarines now helped to guard convoys of merchant ships as they crossed the Atlantic to Europe.

The impact of America entering the war was enormous. For the Allies, it meant huge numbers of new troops and weapons would boost its strength. For Germany, it meant a powerful new enemy to face. The war was about to enter its final phase.

I WANT YOU FOR U.S. ARMY
NEAREST RECRUITING STATION

Posters encouraged young men to enlist in the U.S. Army and Navy.

Carried by British ships, the first American troops arrived

1917: No End in Sight

In February 1917, German forces were given the order to withdraw from their lines in the Somme region on the Western Front. They fell back to a new line, a few miles to the east. The Allies pursued the Germans and by April 1917 the two sides were facing each other again. The scene was set for another year of battles.

Heavy rain and intense shelling turned the area around Passchendaele into a sea of mud.

A German soldier in one of the fortified trenches of the Hindenburg Line, which ran from Arras to Laon in Northern France.

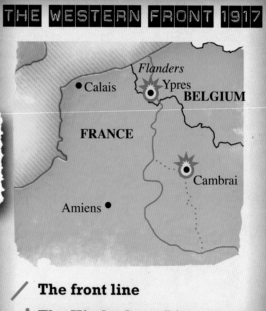

THE WESTERN FRONT 1917

Calais ·   *Flanders*   Ypres   **BELGIUM**

FRANCE

Cambrai ·

Amiens ·

╱ **The front line**

•••• **The Hindenburg Line**

The Hindenburg Line

As the Germans withdrew, they carried out a 'scorched earth' campaign. Anything that might be of use to the Allies was destroyed. Roads, bridges, railway stations and buildings were blown up, villages were set alight, trees were felled, wells were polluted, **mines** and **booby traps** were laid.

The Germans moved to their new line of defences. The British called it the Hindenburg Line. It was 72 kilometres long, but it was not a single line. Instead, it was a defensive zone that stretched back for seven kilometres. Inside the zone were concrete shelters for stormtroopers, machine gun posts, belts of barbed wire 45 metres thick and three lines of trenches. It was the most well-built defence system of the war.

The Third Battle of Ypres

The major battle of the Western Front in 1917 was the Third Battle of Ypres. It became known as Passchendaele (say: pash-en-dale), after the village in Belgium which saw the worst of the fighting. It began with an artillery bombardment. More than 3,000 Allied guns fired four and a half million shells at the German lines. After two weeks, the shelling stopped. Then, at dawn on 31 July, infantry and tanks edged their way across no-man's-land, weaving around shell holes filled with water.

Soldiers used wooden tracks called duckboards to cross the muddy fields of Passchendaele.

The Germans counter-attacked in the afternoon. Shells exploded amongst the advancing Allies and machine gun bullets ripped through them. To make it worse, it began to rain, and very soon the men were knee-deep in mud, and the tanks became stuck.

The rain continued to fall and the trenches filled with water. Conditions were terrible. The Allies had thought the battle would be over in two days. In fact, it lasted ten weeks. In early November, Canadian troops secured the village of Passchendaele – or what was left of it – and the battle ended. More than 500,000 men had been killed or wounded. Of the dead, some were swallowed up by the mud, never to be seen again.

Battle of Cambrai

As winter approached, the Allies planned one final battle of the year – a surpise attack with tanks to break through the Hindenburg Line, near Cambrai. At dawn on 20 November, 381 British tanks rolled forward, spread out along 10km. More than 1,000 artillery pieces launched a creeping barrage, their shells landing in front of the advancing tanks. Behind the tanks were thousands of infantry soldiers.

The Germans were taken by surprise. By the end of the day, the Allies had advanced 8km into German territory, 10,000 prisoners had been captured, and hundreds of guns had been taken. However, a German counter-attack came within days. Many of the British tanks broke down, or were knocked out by grenades. The Germans took back most of the ground they had lost.

British soldiers guide a Mark IV tank over a trench at Cambrai.

War in the Desert

The Allies were defeated at Gallipoli by Turkish forces in 1915 (see page 30). A few months later, in April 1916, British and Indian troops were forced to surrender to the Turks at Kut, a town in Iraq. As Turkey became a force to be reckoned with, Britain decided to act. The plan was to stop Turkey from controlling the Middle East.

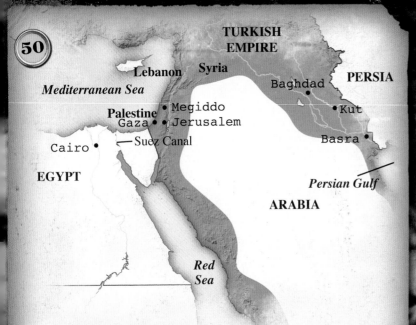

Britain Sends Troops

Britain sent troops to Basra, a town on the Persian Gulf in the south of modern-day Iraq. About 150,000 British and Indian soldiers assembled there. The town was transformed into an army base. A railway and a road were built, and the port and harbour were improved. This made transport and communications better for the army.

The Allies in Egypt

At the same time as Britain was building up its army in Iraq, Allied troops were sent to Egypt. Their role was to defend Egypt and guard the vital supply route of the Suez Canal – a narrow channel of water linking the Mediterranean Sea and the Red Sea. As long as Britain controlled the Suez Canal, it had a 'short cut' to her territories in India, Australia and New Zealand. If the Canal fell into enemy hands, British ships would be forced to take the long route around Africa.

The Invasion of Palestine

By 1917, Allied forces in the Middle East were ready for action against Turkey. That February, British soldiers moved out from their base at Basra and retook Kut from the Turks. From there, they moved north and captured Baghdad without a fight. As the Turkish forces retreated, more towns were captured by the British army.

At the same time as Allied troops were advancing through Iraq, Allied forces moved out of Egypt. Their mission had changed from the defence of Egypt to an all-out attack on Turkish forces in Palestine. To get there, they had to cross the Sinai Desert, with its sandstorms and searing temperatures. In early 1917, two attempts were made to take Gaza, the nearest large town in Palestine. Both attacks failed. In October, the British tried again and in the Third Battle of Gaza, the town was finally taken. By Christmas 1917, Jerusalem was also in British hands.

T.E. Lawrence, later known as Lawrence of Arabia, was a British officer who helped Arab fighters in a guerilla war against the Turks.

The Battle of Megiddo

The final battle for control of the Middle East was at Megiddo in northern Palestine (present-day Israel). Fought in September 1918, it began with a brief artillery bombardment of Turkish defences. French and Indian infantry then advanced and a gap opened up in the Turkish lines. British and Australian cavalry rode through this gap and moved rapidly on to Nazareth. As the Turkish forces retreated, they were bombed and shot at by British planes and more than 1,500 Turkish vehicles were destroyed.

By late October, Allied forces had advanced 480 kilometres across Lebanon and Syria and had taken 75,000 Turkish prisoners and hundreds of guns. Turkish resistance had completely collapsed. On 30 October, Turkey surrendered and the war in the Middle East was over.

ritish troops in shorts
arch through a hot and
usty desert in the
iddle East in 1916.

Turkish prisoners being marched along following their surrender at Megiddo.

Women At War

The First World War changed the lives of women across Europe. As millions of men went off to war, women had to take over their jobs. Women did everything from making munitions, to farm work, factory work, shipbuilding and driving buses. Some joined the army, while others became nurses and tended to wounded soldiers.

Women operating the machines to make bullets in a London munitions factory.

Factory Work

In 1914, at the start of the war, 200,000 women worked in Britain's **munitions** factories, making shells, grenades and bullets. It was dangerous work. By the end of the war, there were 947,000 female munitions workers in Britain. It was the same in Germany. By 1918, more than 700,000 German women were making munitions to send to the troops at the front. Elsewhere, women worked in shipyards, aeroplane factories and coal mines. In textile mills they made military cloth, and in clothing factories they cut and sewed it to make uniforms for the troops.

Recruiting posters encouraged women to join the Women's Land Army.

Farm Work

Across much of Europe, work on the land had always been men's work, but as farmworkers went away to war, women moved in to do their jobs. There were fields to plough and sow with crops, harvests to gather, and animals to tend to. In Britain, there were food shortages as supply ships were sunk by German submarines. It meant more food had to be produced at home, and 250,000 women went to work on the country's farms. Many of them joined the Women's Land Army. Women also worked on the farm fields of France, and in the closing months of the war some men were brought back from the front line to work on the land.

Women in the Army

Women also joined the army. In Russia, the Women's Battalion of Death was formed. This was a fighting unit of the Russian army, with about 300 women soldiers. They shaved their heads, wore the same uniforms as men and saw action against German forces on the Eastern Front.

Other countries also had women soldiers, but they had non-combat roles. In Britain, women in the Women's Army Auxiliary Corps were sent to the front to work as cooks, signallers, clerks, truck and ambulance drivers. These were jobs men had done, but with women doing the jobs, men were freed up to fight at the front.

Members of the Women's Army Auxiliary Corps during drill practice in London, 1917.

Nurses at War

Women nurses served close to the front line in the war zones. They worked at wound-dressing stations, which were set up as near to the fighting as possible. The nurses cared for injured men who were rushed to them, many with terrible injuries. From there, women drove ambulances, taking the injured to field hospitals set up away from the fighting in disused barracks and schools, in convents, railway stations and shattered buildings. More nurses cared for the injured on board ambulance trains and ships as they were taken back to their home countries.

Wounded French and British soldiers being treated by a nurse.

1918: The Last Great Battles

From August 1914, the war in Europe had been fought on two fronts – the Western Front and the Eastern Front. The forces of Germany and Austria-Hungary lay between these fronts, surrounded by enemy countries. That was until December 1917, when Russia, as a result of internal divisions and revolutions, decided to leave the war. Russia signed a peace **treaty** with Germany, so German troops were no longer needed on the Eastern Front. More than one million German soldiers and 3,000 guns were moved across to the Western Front.

Germany's Great Push Forward

In the spring of 1918, German forces on the Western Front were in a strong position to mount a major attack from along the Hindenburg Line. Reinforced with men from the Eastern Front, German forces outnumbered the Allies. Germany wanted to break through the Allied lines before American troops arrived in large numbers.

The German attack began at dawn on 21 March. It was along a front line in north-east France that stretched for 65km. The Germans sent 6,500 big guns, 3,500 mortars, 730 planes and 750,000 men into action against a British force half the size. It was the biggest attack of the war, but that wasn't all – the Germans also changed their battle tactics. Instead of a massive bombardment lasting for days, they opened with a short, heavy barrage. When the shelling stopped, thousands of German infantrymen swarmed rapidly towards the British lines.

German troops wait in their trenches at the start of the spring offensive.

Paris under Fire

The British forces were overwhelmed by wave after wave of German troops coming at them. The British retreated, as did the French when their positions were attacked. The rapid German advance continued and thousands of British and French soldiers were taken prisoner. Soon, Paris was in range of the Germans' giant 'Paris Gun'. This massive weapon had a barrel 40 metres long and was the biggest gun of the war. Between March and August 1918, it fired more than 300 shells, hitting the city from 130 kilometres away. For Germany, everything seemed to be going according to plan.

The Paris Gun was a huge converted naval gun mounted on a railway truck.

The Germans Retreat

By June 1918, the German advance towards Paris had gone as far as it could. German forces had come to a stop. The men were hungry, as it was taking a long time for supplies to reach the troops, and thousands were also suffering from flu. In July, the Allies began to fight back, and for the first time, large numbers of American troops went into action. The Germans began to retreat.

Two German soldiers surrender near Soissons in nothern France in 1918.

American infantry troops go over the top during an attack on the Western Front in 1918.

The 100 Days Offensive

For the next 100 days, the Allies were on the attack. German forces were defeated in three quick battles – the Second Battle of the Marne (July), the Battle of Amiens (August), and the Second Battle of the Somme (August). The Germans retreated to their defences along the Hindenburg Line, but in September and October the Allies broke through. The German army began to collapse. Thousands of men laid down their arms and surrendered. The end of the war was in sight.

1918: The War Ends

One by one, Germany's war allies stopped fighting. Their armies could no longer carry on, so they agreed to an **armistice** – to lay down their arms, to stop fighting and begin peace talks. The first to surrender was Bulgaria, at the end of September 1918. Then Turkey agreed to a ceasefire at the end of October. A few days later, in the first week of November, Austria-Hungary agreed to a **truce**. This left Germany as the only country still at war with the Allies.

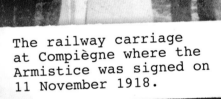

The railway carriage at Compiègne where the Armistice was signed on 11 November 1918.

British soldiers escort a column of German priosners near the Somme in 1918.

Germany Surrenders

By early November 1918, the Allies had broken through the German lines on the Western Front. As the German army was pushed back, its soldiers lost the will to fight. German sailors refused to go back to sea and in Germany itself there were riots in the cities, brought on by a shortage of food. Germany had lost the support of its allies and it was now only a matter of time before it admitted defeat.

On 9 November, a group of high-ranking German officials travelled to the Forest of Compiègne in north-east France. They met officers from Britain and France, who presented them with an armistice document – the orders for the surrender of Germany. The German government was given three days to accept it.

The Fighting Stops

After nearly three days of talks, Germany signed the armistice document at five o'clock on the morning of 11 November 1918. It was signed in a railway carriage in the Forest of Compiègne. Both sides agreed that the war would stop six hours later, at eleven o'clock – the eleventh hour of the eleventh day of the eleventh month.

During those final six hours of war, gunshots still rang out along the Western Front. Men from both sides were killed right up to the last minute. But then, at eleven o'clock, the guns fell silent. After four years of fighting, it was finally all quiet on the Western Front. And when German forces fighting in East Africa surrendered on 23 November, the war to end all wars was finally over.

Evening Standard

LATE NIGHT SPECIAL

LONDON, MONDAY, NOVEMBER 11, 1918.   ONE PENNY.

END OF THE WAR

GERMANY SIGNS OUR TERMS & FIGHTING STOPPED AT 11 O'CLOCK TO-DAY.

ALLIES TRIUMPHANT. FULL ARMISTICE TERMS

...CH AND LLOYD GEORGE TELL NEWS EVACUATION TO THE RHINE AND
SENT THE WORLD REJOICING.   BRIDGEHEADS FOR ALLIES

1919: A New Europe

After the war had ended, the countries involved signed peace treaties. In 1919, Germany signed the Treaty of Versailles. It said that the German army could have no more than 100,000 troops and that Germany had to pay the Allies for damage caused during the war. Also, Germany's borders were changed. The border regions of Alsace and Lorraine, taken from France in 1870–71, were handed back (see page 4). Germans thought the Treaty was too harsh. Britain and France thought that Germany had got away lightly.

Austria-Hungary signed treaties that split up its empire, creating the separate countries of Austria and Hungary. The new countries of Czechoslovakia and Yugoslavia were also created and the map of Europe was redrawn.

Sinking the German Fleet

After Germany had surrendered, her fleet of warships sailed to the British naval base at Scapa Flow, Orkney, Scotland. The fleet's German commander feared he would to be ordered to hand the ships over to the British, but rather than do this, he gave the order to sink the fleet. On 21 June 1919, a total of 52 ships were sent to the bottom of the sea.

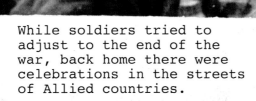

While soldiers tried to adjust to the end of the war, back home there were celebrations in the streets of Allied countries.

The German ship *Bayern* sinks beneath the waves at Scapa Flow.

Animals at War

Animals played an important part in the war. They risked their lives and countless millions died as they served the armed forces of both sides. Different animals were chosen for their natural skills and instincts. They carried out difficult and dangerous jobs, often in extreme conditions. Animals are the forgotten army of the war.

Two Allied soldiers sending a message by carrier pigeon in Belgium 1915.

Carrier Pigeons

Tens of thousands of carrier pigeons carried messages for their countries, in small tubes attached to their legs. The messages were in code, which the enemy could not read if it fell into their hands. When the first British tanks went into battle in 1916, they took carrier pigeons with them. The tanks were so noisy inside that it was impossible to hear messages sent by radio – pigeons were the only way to communicate with headquarters.

A sergeant from a British signals section puts a message into the metal cylinder attached to the collar of a messenger dog.

Dogs of War

Dogs were used by both sides to carry messages between the trenches, in tubes attached to their collars. Because they were small and moved fast, snipers found these dog messengers very hard to shoot. Some dogs were trained to pull small carts filled with ammunition and supplies, which they took to the troops at the front line. At night, dogs used their strong sense of smell to sniff out wounded soldiers stranded in no-man's-land, before guiding stretcher-bearers to them.

A British army camel caravan treks through the desert.

Camels

In the deserts of the Middle East, British, Australian and New Zealand forces used 5,000 camels to transport men, equipment and supplies. They were also ridden into battle by infantry soldiers. Camels were the ideal animals for war in the desert, as they could travel long distances over sand and go for days without water.

War Horses

Horses were the main war animal used in the First World War, as they had been for hundreds of years. However, this was the last war in which cavalry soldiers and their war horses charged into battle. The battlefields of the Western Front were no place for the mounted troops of the cavalry, who were easily cut down by machine gun fire or stopped by deep shell holes and barbed wire. Instead, horses were mainly used to carry messages and to pull guns, supply wagons, field kitchens and ambulances.

By 1917, Britain had more than one million horses in service. By the time the war was over, more than eight million horses from both sides had died. On just one day, during the Battle of Verdun in 1916, 7,000 horses were killed by shells fired by French and German guns.

A horse pulls a railway cart loaded with wounded British soldiers along tracks from the front line to a dressing station.

Legacy of War

The First World War ended almost 100 years ago, but it is not forgotten today. Between 1914 and 1918, millions of young men were killed in action, more were badly injured and millions of people became refugees. A generation of young men had died. In the years that followed, and right up to the present day, the legacy of this terrible conflict is still there for us to see and to remember.

Memorials for the Dead

At eight o'clock every evening, the 'Last Post' is sounded by buglers at the Menin Gate Memorial to the Missing, in Ypres, Belgium. Carved in stone on the panels of this huge arch are the names of 54,896 British and Commonwealth soldiers who were killed in the fighting around Ypres. As their bodies were never found, they could never be laid to rest in a war cemetery. For these missing men, this is the place to remember them.

After the war, millions of fallen men were laid to rest in peaceful cemeteries close to the battlefields that claimed their young lives. In their home towns, war memorials were put up in public places, recording the names of those who gave their lives for their countries.

Remembrance Day Poppies

After the war, it was noticed that the red corn poppy was one of the few plants that would grow on the churned-up battlefields of northern France and the Flanders region of Belgium. In 1920, the red poppy was chosen as the national symbol of remembrance in the USA. The following year, it also became the national symbol in Britain. Today, on the 11 November each year, people in Britain, Canada, Australia, New Zealand, South Africa and the USA wear poppies on Remembrance Day, which is known as Veteran's Day in the USA.

A piper plays at the Menin Gate to honour the memory of the thousands of British and Commonwealth soldiers killed in the First World War.

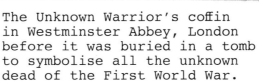

Unknown Soldiers

In London, Paris, Brussels and Arlington, USA, a dead soldier from each country was laid to rest in that country's Tomb of the Unknown Soldier. These soldiers were specifically chosen because they could not be identified. Each one represents all the unidentified and missing soldiers who died for their country in the war.

The Unknown Warrior's coffin in Westminster Abbey, London before it was buried in a tomb to symbolise all the unknown dead of the First World War.

Archaeology of War

Beneath the fields of the Western Front, the remains of the war lie buried. Trenches, tunnels, unexploded shells, weapons and the bones of fallen soldiers are all still there. They are sometimes accidentally brought to light when farmers plough the land, or during building work. Some are found by archaeologists, as happened in 1998 at Flesquières, France, when a British tank from the Battle of Cambrai was discovered buried in a pit.

In 2009, archaeologists recovered the remains of 250 soldiers from a mass grave at Fromelles, France. They had been killed on 19 July 1916 in the Battle of Fromelles. Most of the dead were Australian and a few were British. Some were identified from their personal possessions. Others were identified by using DNA analysis to trace descendants who are alive today. All the dead were reburied in 2010 in a new war cemetery nearby.

The British Mark IV tank that was recovered at Flesquières shows the battle damage caused by German artillery fire.

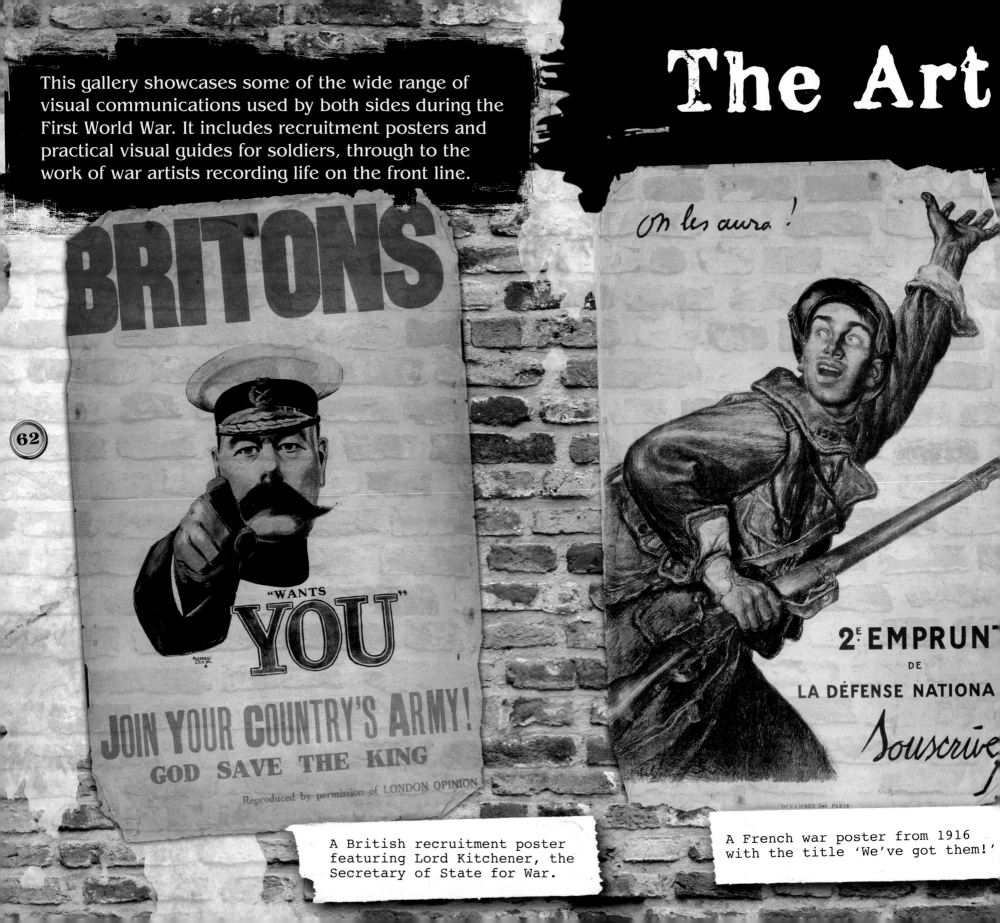

This gallery showcases some of the wide range of visual communications used by both sides during the First World War. It includes recruitment posters and practical visual guides for soldiers, through to the work of war artists recording life on the front line.

62

A British recruitment poster featuring Lord Kitchener, the Secretary of State for War.

A French war poster from 1916 with the title 'We've got them!'

A soldier gestures towards a queue of volunteers in this German recruitment poster.

An American recruitment poster for the U.S. Marines from 1918.

SOUTH AUSTRALIANS

COO-EE!

FALL IN!

WE WANT **YOU** AT THE FRONT

COME AND HELP
ENLIST AT ONCE

A recruitment poster calling for South Australians to enlist.

An Italian poster from 1917 declares that 'Everyone must do their duty'.

Fate tutti il vostro dovere!

LE SOTTOSCRIZIONI AL PRESTITO SI RICEVONO PRESSO IL CREDITO ITALIANO

64

A Canadian poster recruiting sailors for the navy.

65

A Russian poster calling for funds to support the war against Germany in 1917.

A German wallchart from 1914 showing the uniforms of Allied soldiers, including French, Belgian and British troops.

A French poster from 1915, providing a recognition guide to the various uniforms of the German army.

Artists from both sides tried to capture the horrific realities of war in their art. This picture of soldiers at the front is by Gunner F.J. Mears, who served in the British artillery.

Glossary

Alliance
A group of countries or people who come together to support each other.

Airships
A type of aircraft that floated like a balloon because they were filled with hydrogen gas.

Armistice
An agreement to stop fighting and begin peace talks; a truce.

Artillery
Large guns used in fighting on land.

Assassinate
To kill an important person.

Barbed wire
Wire with spikes, used to make fences and barriers.

Barrage
An artillery attack with heavy and continuous gunfire.

Bayonet
A stabbing knife fixed to the end of a rifle.

Blockaded
When a place, such as a port, is sealed off to prevent goods or people from entering or leaving.

Bombardment
A barrage of heavy and continuous artillery gunfire.

Booby traps
Devices meant to kill or injure a person.

Chlorine
A greenish-yellow coloured poisonous gas.

Conscripted
Conscripted soldiers are those who have been ordered to join the armed forces, instead of those who have volunteered.

Eastern Front
The name of the battle line in Eastern Europe.

Fronts
The war zone; the places where the fighting actually happens.

Heir
A person who inherits something, such as property or a title, from another person.

Howitzers
A type of big gun that fires shells at a steep angle, high into the sky.

Infantry
Soldiers who fight on foot.

'Land ship'
The original name given to a tank.

Mines
Types of hidden bomb, used on land or at sea.

Mobilised
When troops are made ready to fight in a war.

Mortars
Small guns that fire shells very quickly from the trenches.

Munitions
Weapons and ammunition.

Non-combatants
Service people not directly involved in combat, e.g. bearers or army doctors and medical orderlies.

No-man's-land
The land that lay between the two sides.

Over the top
When soldiers left the safety of a trench, hoisting themselves up and climbing out of it.

Shells
Ammunition for artillery weapons, made from a metal case filled with explosive and designed to be fired from a big gun e.g. a howitzer.

Shrapnel
Jagged pieces of metal from exploding shells.

Stalemate
When neither side has an advantage; a draw.

Tanks
Heavy, armour-plated vehicles with caterpillar tracks and one or more guns.

Torpedo
An underwater missile fired from a submarine.

Treaty
An agreement to do something, made between countries or people.

Trenches
A series of long and narrow ditches dug into the ground.

Truce
An agreement to stop fighting, sometimes leading to peace talks and an armistice.

Western Front
The name of the main battle line in Western Europe.

70

The publishers would like to thank the following sources for their kind permission to reproduce the pictures in this book.

Key: t = top, b = bottom, l = left, r = right & c = centre

AKG-Images: 20, 28b, 28tr, 30b, 36-37, 37br, 39br, /IAM: 29br, /Interfoto: 20b, 28r, 29c, /MPortfolio/Electa: 15br, /Jean-Pierre Verney: 28l, 63l, 67
Alamy: Art Archive: 43b, 53tr, 53br, /Interfoto: 13cr, 43r, 21l, 21tl, 26-27, /Lyroky: 37tr, /Military Images: 13l, /SOTK2011: 37tr, /Pictorial Press: 62l, /Western Front Images: 61br
Bridgeman Art Library: /Archives Charmet: 42tr, 65l, /Moore-Gwyn Fine Art: 68-69, /Peter Newark Pictures: 26br, /Universal History Archive/UIG: 12b
Carlton Books: Specially photographed with kind permission from Imperial War Museums, London: 66
Corbis: 41l, 46t, /adoc-photos: 23r, /Bettmann: 6-7, 7b, 10-11, 24-25, 54-55, /Fine Art Photographic Library: 4, /Christel Gerstenberg: 5b, 9b, /Hulton-Deutsch Collection: 11t, 24bl, 25br, 58tr, /George H. Mewes/National Geographic Society: 16l, /National Geographic Society: 58br, /Underwood &Underwood: 49br
DK Images: /Geoff Dann: 23l, /Gary Ombler/Courtesy of the Board of Trustees of the Royal Armouries: 13tr
Getty: 5c, 7t, 8, 11c, 12-13, 13b, 17r, 26l, 29tr, 32-33, 33l, 34bl, 35tr, 38-39, 40-41, 41br, 48-49, 50-51, 64r, /IWM: 43t, 58l, /Mondadori: 16-17, /Popperfoto: 19r, 25tr, 34-35, 48l, /Time & Life Pictures: 9t, 32bl, 38l, 63r, /Roger Viollet: 18-19, 20-21
Imperial War Museum: 15tr, 22, 29tc, 33tr, 35l **Mary Evans:** /Epic/Tallandier: 21br, /Robert Hunt Library: 14l, 17b, 23br, 24br, /Illustrated London News Ltd: 14-15, 22l
Photo12: /Ann Ronan Picture Library: 22br
Topfoto.co.uk: 30-31, 42bl, 45br, 47t, 49tr, 51br, 52l, 52b, 52-53, 55b, 56l, 56r, 57l, 57tr, 59, 60-61, 61tr, 64l, /Granger Collection: 46b, 47br, 51t, /Print Collector/HIP: 55r, 61tl, /The Image Works: 2-3, /Ullstein Bild: 31r, 35r, 42br, 44-45, 57br, 70-71, /Roger Viollet: 21r, 35b, 47bl, /World History Archive: 65r,
Wiki Media Commons: 16bl, 37bl

Every effort has been made to acknowledge correctly and contact the source and/or copyright holder of each picture and Carlton Books Limited apologises for any unintentional errors or omissions, which will be corrected in future editions of this book.